WALKING WITH
EPHESIANS

BECOMING THE MAN GOD INTENDS YOU TO BE

A 30-DAY DEVOTIONAL
AND BIBLE STUDY

FRED J. PARRY

From the author of *Walking with James*
Becoming the Man God Intends You to Be

WALKING WITH EPHESIANS

Interior Page Design by Carolyn Preul
Copy Editing by Lisa Thornton Stillwell
Technical Review by Bob Walz
ISBN: 978-1-7923-2685-1

ACKNOWLEDGMENT:
Special thanks to my friend, Bob Walz, for his steadfast guidance and
counsel during the writing and editing of *Walking With James* and
Walking With Ephesians. More than just encouraging me through the writing
process, Bob has given me a more complete understanding of the nature of
God and, for that, I will be forever indebted. Bob is a divisional leader for the
Navigators organization. Bob is based in Lincoln, Nebraska, where he has
invested in thousands of young Christians for more than 40 years. Bob and
his wife, Sandy, have four grown children and four grandchildren.
Bob loves studying and sharing God's Word. He has a website that has
many tools to help others get into the Word (www.dscplwrx.com).

FOR MY BEAUTIFUL WIFE, MELODY

"Many women do noble things, but you surpass them all."
(Proverbs 31:29)

CONTENTS

For more information on using this book for a group study,
please visit www.FredParry.Life for study materials, handouts,
and other useful information.

INTRODUCTION

For we are God's handiwork, created in Christ Jesus to do good works, which God prepared in advance for us to do. (Ephesians 2:10)

If you're like me, you have probably experienced more than your fair share of doubts about your worthiness as a Christian. As a man, I have always struggled with temptation, pride, greed, and an unseemly tendency to place myself before God and others. Rather than confronting my brokenness and the deep-seated wounds of my past, I worked diligently to hide my pain and shortcomings behind a facade of confidence, humor, and unbecoming behavior. I suspect that my situation is not unique.

Now that I have grown spiritually, I am beginning to recognize the incredible gift of God's grace and the generous inheritance that He has planned for me. With this new understanding, I am slowly gaining the confidence I need to let my guard down and give my imperfections the light of day. Paul's letter to the Ephesians is, in many respects, a "must-read" for men as it gives tremendous insight into the remarkable relationship we have with our loving God and how we should relate to Him as Christians.

In many respects, Paul's life offers a powerful example of hope and redemption. A close study of his time on this earth reveals what it means to live a transformed life. From his early days of persecuting followers of Christ to his remarkable encounter with Jesus on the road to Damascus, we get to witness God's grace and mercy at work. In the end, Paul would rise to become a remarkably important figure in the growth of Christianity.

Paul's letter to the Ephesians is rich with Biblical doctrine and a great reminder that merely being a good person and obeying the Ten Commandments is not enough. Paul calls us to grow in our spiritual maturity, encouraging us to up our game in the way that we love each other, honor our marriages, and protect our hearts and minds from the work of the devil. Through all of this, we get a better understanding of God's true nature and how our walk can honor Him.

If you get nothing else from Paul's letter to the Ephesians, you should, at the very least, heed his advice regarding the threat of spiritual warfare. Paul writes that we should put on the "Armor of God" so that we can defend ourselves against the devil's relentless attempts to pull us away from God and destroy our lives. Paul warns us to never let our guard down when it comes to the work of the Evil One. Although it may seem counter-intuitive, the closer we get to God, the stronger the devil's pull will become and the greater his attacks.

Although Paul's writings are more than 2,000 years old, his wisdom transcends time and resonates with modern-day readers in remarkable ways. For example, Paul's call for unity between Jews and Gentiles living in Ephesus is remarkably poignant and eerily similar to the message we might receive in modern times regarding the discourse that still exists between blacks and whites in the United States and in South Africa as well as between the Israelis and Palestinians in Gaza.

Paul was not a perfect man, and for that reason alone, he is relatable and there is much to learn from his writings and the lessons he shared with the first generation of Christians. As men, we can benefit from his timeless wisdom on grace, acceptance, and what it means to be a life-giving husband.

It is my prayer that you, too, will find hope and wisdom in the words of Paul and in the devotionals written here that have been inspired by his letter to the Ephesians. Because the best way to grow spiritually is to do so in community with other men, I hope that you'll consider inviting another man or group of men to do this study with you. As iron sharpens iron, one man sharpens another. (Proverbs 27:17)

We are indeed God's handiwork, called to do good works because God gave us a great honor by choosing us to be a part of his family. We can rest assured that as we grow in our knowledge of God's word, we will also grow in His love, a love that is fortified by His gift of the Holy Spirit.

Fred J. Parry

HOW TO USE THIS BOOK

alking with Ephesians is designed to serve the dual
purpose of being a daily devotional and a Bible study
guide for Paul's Epistle to the Ephesians. While the
book is structured to be used over a six-week period, I would
encourage you to use it at a pace that is most comfortable for
you.

Each of the daily devotions is inspired by one of Paul's
messages in this important letter that encourages unity and
keeping the Church pure and holy. From these messages,
I have found themes that can guide us in our daily walk to
become better Christians. These devotionals were written as
responses from my own personal understanding of how a
particular verse spoke to me. The goal of any Bible study is
to find the correct interpretation which leads to a variety of
applications. That, in itself, is rightly handling the word of
truth. (2 Timothy 2:15)

If you're like me, you'll get a new insight or meaning each time
you read one of these passages and not because the Bible's
meaning has changed, but because we, as individuals, have
changed since the last time we were there. We've become more
aware of a different aspect of our lives, and this Scripture now
speaks to us in a new way. We are more teachable than we were

before. The Bible takes us on where we are, and God uses His Word to lead us to greater maturity and a broader perspective. The Bible is as deep as we are and deeper still.

I would suggest approaching each devotional in prayer, asking God for clarity of mind and focus with the hope that the day's message resonates with you in some meaningful way.

Once you've read the devotional, you'll find the following tools at the end of each reading to help you get the most meaning out of the day's message:

- a reference to Scripture outside Ephesians that will reinforce and add context to the day's message.

- next, you'll find two short questions designed to help you apply that day's lesson to your life.

- finally, you'll find a call to contemplation which is intended as a prompt for journaling. It's an excellent opportunity to explore and record your feelings as they relate to the day's message.

In the coming pages, you'll find the complete text of the Epistle to the Ephesians reprinted with permission of Biblica, Inc. To gain a better understanding of the literary and cultural context of each day's passage, I would encourage you to refer to the full text each day to fully understand the contextual circumstances and events surrounding each passage.

I hope that you'll find these devotionals to be useful and relevant in your daily walk. My prayer is that the wisdom that comes from Paul's Letter to the Ephesians will guide you in your journey to lead a more fulfilling and Christ-centered life

FJP

MY PRAYER

Father, God, I pray that I will be blessed with the clarity of mind and a willing heart as I begin this study of Paul's letter to the Ephesians. God, give me the courage of Paul to explore each message with confidence and affirmation that You have indeed set aside an inheritance like none other for me. God, use this opportunity to teach me about love and unity and to help me grasp the depth and breadth of the salvation you've guaranteed for me. Let what I learn allow me to serve You by serving others. I pray for these things in the name of Your Son and our Savior, Jesus Christ. Amen.

BACKGROUND

ABOUT EPHESUS

Ephesus was once an ancient port city on the Aegean Sea in what is now considered modern-day Turkey. Through various points in history, Ephesus was a city of great significance because of its location along major trade routes through the Mediterranean region and because the city, itself, was once the center for cultural and educational activity.

Archaeological evidence suggests this region was first inhabited during the Neolithic Age, almost 6,000 years before the birth of Christ. When Alexander the Great first visited Ephesus in 334 B.C., he took a special interest in a temple being built to honor the Greek goddess Artemis. The temple had been under construction for more than 120 years. Alexander offered to finance the completion of the temple, suggesting it be named in his honor. The Ephesians, hoping to persuade him otherwise, played to Alexander's ego by telling him he was essentially the equivalent of a god and, therefore, it would be inappropriate for one god to build a temple in honor of another god. He eventually lost interest in the project.

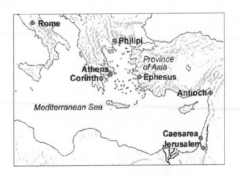

The temple's namesake, Artemis, was the goddess of the hunt, chastity, childbirth, wild animals and fertility. Romans often referred to this same deity as Diana. This matron goddess was perhaps the most honored of all deities. Statues of Artemis show a woman with multiple breasts, which no doubt contributed to her popularity. Replicas of the goddess were quite popular with visitors who traveled through Ephesus.

The temple honoring her was completely rebuilt on three separate occasions. The final version of the temple, which was destroyed by The Goths in A.D. 263, measured 418' x 239' and featured 100 giant marble columns as part of its design. Once completed, it was nearly four times the size of the Parthenon. It was so large that it was named as one of the Seven Wonders of the World.

When Caesar Augustus was the Emperor of Rome (27 B.C. through A.D. 12), Ephesus became a seat for the Roman governor and hence, the capital of all of Asia Minor. Ephesus was an important city in Biblical history because the apostle Paul visited Ephesus on three separate occasions. On his second trip there in A.D. 52, he stayed for three years. There, Paul preached that the one true God was not made by human hands (Acts 19:23-41) and therefore they should no longer purchase shrines and artifacts used in the worship of Diana. This, of course, affected those whose business it was to make these souvenirs of false idols. Acts 19 tells the story of Paul and his encounter with a vendor named Demetrius who made silver coins in the likeness of Artemis. Demetrius convinced a large crowd to revolt against Paul and his disciples and planned a riot against them. Many of these merchants did all they could to prevent Christianity from getting a foothold in the region. They knew it would eventually end the sales of these false idols.

Although the city itself has essentially vanished, Ephesus is still among the most significant Roman archaeological sites in the world. Historians believe that Mary, the mother of Jesus, spent her final years in Ephesus as did the apostle John, the only apostle who did not die a martyr's death. Visitors to this region can now visit the home where Mary is believed to have lived and the Basilica of St. John above the site where John is believed to have been buried on Ayasuluk Hill.

Today, the ruins of this once-great city can be found about 50 miles south of Izmir, Turkey and six miles inland from the Aegean Sea. Because of the city's significance in the history of Christianity, the area is now a popular destination for Christian pilgrimages.

THE APOSTLE PAUL

Paul was born in the city of Tarsus, a major city in eastern Cilicia on the trade route between Syria and Asia Minor. Born the son of a Pharisee and in the ancestral lineage of the Tribe of Benjamin, Paul enjoyed the unique distinction of being a Jew and the privilege of being a Roman citizen. He could speak Hebrew but his native tongue was Koine Greek. Paul was educated at the prestigious Rabbinical school taught by Gamaliel, who is thought to be one of the most influential Rabbis in the history of ancient Judaism.

Next to Jesus, Paul is considered the second most important figure in the history and growth of Christianity. He is believed to be the author of 13 of the 27 books in the New Testament. While there is some scholarly debate as to the complete authenticity of this claim, experts acknowledge that at least seven of these 13 books are undisputed as authentic works of Paul. Some scholars speculate that his Epistle to the Ephesians may have been written as much as 20 years after his death by one of his loyal understudies. They point to evidence related to the sentence structure in the letter and the fact that Ephesus is not mentioned in the earliest manuscripts of this Epistle. However, the themes and messages in the letter are consistent with Paul's teachings at the time. In addition to his own writings in the New Testament, nearly half of the Book of Acts is also dedicated to the historical accounts of Paul's life and his works.

Readers of the New Testament first encounter Paul while he was still known as Saul of Tarsus. Although Saul was a tentmaker by trade, he was also a fervent persecutor of the disciples and early followers of Jesus. Biblical scholars describe Paul's physical stature as a short man with a bald head and crooked legs. In Acts 9:1-22, we read of Saul traveling from Jerusalem to Damascus to arrest disciples when he encounters the resurrected Jesus in a great light. During this experience, Jesus reveals to Saul that He is Lord and that in persecuting His followers Saul is the same as persecuting the Lord Jesus and is, in effect, fighting against God. During this encounter, Saul was blinded by the light but he traveled on to Damascus where he remained blind for three days. Saul took no food or water for this period of time and stayed in a constant state of prayer until approached by a disciple named

Ananias who told him that he had been sent by Jesus to restore his sight and that the Lord would fill him with the Holy Spirit. Once Saul's sight was restored, he was immediately baptized and became a fervent follower, and believer, in Jesus Christ.

Following his baptism by Ananias, Paul went on to Arabia and Damascus and began to preach that Jesus was indeed the Messiah. It was soon thereafter that he, himself, began to be persecuted for his teachings. Around A.D. 37, nearly three years after his conversion, Paul traveled to Jerusalem where he met for 15 days with James, the half-brother of Jesus, and Simon Peter. Paul used these meetings to learn more about the life of Jesus and to report on his efforts in preaching about the Kingdom of God and Jesus the Messiah. Over time, Paul became known as the "Apostle to the Gentiles," while Peter was known as the "Apostle to the Jews."

Soon after Paul met with James and Simon Peter, he returned to his hometown of Tarsus to preach until he was invited by Barnabas to go and teach in Antioch. It was there where Paul began to build a network of house churches in which the earliest Christians would gather at the homes of other followers until the size of the group forced them to divide into smaller groups and to meet at multiple homes. With limited resources, Paul and Barnabas often relied on the generosity of their converts for food and housing. In A.D. 47, Paul returned to Jerusalem with Barnabas and brought famine relief, which was contributed by the early churches they had started. In this respect, Paul was, perhaps, the earliest pioneer of missionary work that would be done by churches in the coming centuries.

Paul and Barnabas then set out from Antioch on the first of three mission trips. During the first trip, they visited Cyprus and Galatia. Hoping to build unity between Jews and Gentiles for the benefit of God's kingdom, Paul attended the Council of Jerusalem in A.D. 49 to successfully argue that Gentiles should not be required to follow Jewish Law in order to become Christians. It is around this time in scripture where Saul begins being referenced as Paul. Historians speculate that Paul was actually Saul's Roman name and that the names may have been used interchangeably for a period of time so that he could more easily relate to a diverse variety of audiences.

On his second missionary trip, Paul traveled with Silas through Asia Minor and Greece and settled in Corinth, where it is believed he wrote his letter to the Thessalonians. After short stints in Jerusalem and Antioch, Paul began his third missionary trip and settled in Ephesus.

In Ephesus, Paul wrote his Epistles to the Galatians and Corinthians. He stayed in Ephesus for three years and built strong relationships using this central location and heavily traveled trade routes to spread Christianity through a vast region. Armed with the Holy Spirit and his ability to relate well with both Jews and Gentiles, Paul went on to start several churches throughout Asia Minor, Europe, and the Roman Empire. Along the way, the Lord performed a number of miracles through Paul including healing a crippled man at Lystra (Acts 14:8-18), raising Eutychus from the dead in Troas (Acts 20:8-12), and healing a woman who had been possessed by an evil spirit (Acts 16:18).

Over the course of his ministry life, Paul was jailed on numerous occasions and placed under house arrest for extended periods of time. It was during these periods that Paul crafted several of his letters to the churches he had planted. Because these letters were written while he was imprisoned, they are often referred to as the "Captivity Epistles." In Acts 16:16-34, we read that Paul and Silas were imprisoned in Philippi for disturbing the peace after casting a demon out of a slave girl. While imprisoned, a sudden earthquake brought down the walls of the jail. Paul and Silas did not escape and this led to establishing a trusted relationship with their jailer, who became a follower of Christ. In A.D. 57, Paul returned to Jerusalem and was later arrested and jailed for taking a Gentile too far into the precincts of the temple.

During his captivity in Jerusalem, Paul defended his actions before the Sanhedrin. His testimony divided the Sadducees and Pharisees who had strong disagreements over whether Paul had broken any laws. Paul then requested that his case be heard by Caesar. After his request was reluctantly granted, Paul was placed on a ship, as a prisoner, to sail to Rome. On that voyage, he was shipwrecked on the island of Malta for three months where he performed miracles and continued to preach the word of God. When he finally arrived in Rome, Paul was placed under house arrest but was allowed to continue preaching without interruption from authorities. During this time, Paul wrote his letters to the Philippians, Ephesians, Colossians, and Philemon. Upon his release, it is believed that Paul then traveled to Spain during which time he wrote his letters to Timothy and Titus.

In A.D. 64, Paul returned to Rome where he was martyred. While little has been written regarding the details surrounding Paul's death, tradition has it that Paul was sentenced to death by the Roman Emperor Nero. Paul's death sentence came shortly after a large portion of Rome had burned in a fire. Nero blamed the fire on Christians. Because Paul was a Roman citizen, he was exempt from death by crucifixion. Instead, he was decapitated by a sword. In the end, Paul died because of his faith. In his final writings, it was clear that Paul was ready and willing to die for Christ; giving his last breath for the cause of helping the first generation of Christians understand that sacrifice was an essential part of following Christ.

PAUL'S LETTER TO EPHESUS

Paul wrote his Epistle to Ephesus in A.D. 62 while he was under house arrest in Rome. It is the tenth book of the New Testament. His familiarity and awareness of the Ephesians was a result of his three visits to Ephesus. As was mentioned previously, there is some debate over whether or not Paul was the actual author of this letter; however, there is little doubt that the key thoughts and beliefs introduced in this writing reflect exactly what was on Paul's heart.

Upon closer examination of this letter, it appears as if the six chapters are divided into two distinct parts. The first three chapters describe what our relationship with God should look like and what we should know and believe about this relationship. The final three chapters focus on our relationships with others and how we should live out our lives as Christians. God's love and authority are revealed in this letter with its emphasis through the

illustration of the unique relationship He had with Christ, with
Paul, and with the Gentiles.

In its sum total, the purpose of the Epistle to the Ephesians was
to remind new Christians about the truths of God's work through
Christ, the church and through the diverse people living in the
region. The letter also places an emphasis on the conduct by
which we should abide at home, in the church, and in the world.

Another central theme was Paul's admonition to newly converted
Jews who often separated themselves from Gentiles because they
believed them to be morally deficient. Jews, at the time, were
openly critical of the Gentiles' tendencies toward idolatry and
other behaviors that they believed made them unwashed and
unworthy.

**The following is a summary of the key themes introduced in
each chapter:**

Chapter 1 covers the spiritual blessings that have been given to
us as followers of Christ. Paul tells us that we have been set aside
for God's purposes and that God has made each of us holy and
blameless. God has not only given us the gift of the Holy Spirit
but He has set aside an eternal inheritance for us.

Chapter 2 discusses our salvation through God. We are
disobedient and sinful, and the devil has great influence over
our every move. God raised each of us up by His own grace and
reminds us of our need for reconciliation with others. It is made
known that our salvation is entirely of God's doing rather than

something we have earned. We were not saved by our works but by His grace. We have been called to live as His workmanship out of gratefulness for His gifts.

Chapter 3 reminds us that both Jews and Gentiles will share equally in the inheritance promised by God. God's love is deep and wide and the same should be true about our love for others.

Chapter 4 provides instructions on how we should live out our Christian faith. We must have a desire to become spiritually mature and live with integrity in all that we do. We should cast away our anger and not grieve the Holy Spirit.

Chapter 5 instructs us to live in submission to one another. Wives should submit to their husbands, who in turn, should submit themselves to God and love their wives the way Christ loved his church. Children are instructed to submit to their parents and slaves should submit to their masters. Masters are reminded to treat their slaves with dignity because all men will have a master in heaven. Paul uses this chapter to explain the value of sacrificial love and the importance of giving oneself for the benefit of others.

Chapter 6 teaches us about our need to be prepared for spiritual warfare. The devil is always scheming against us and we must be prepared at all times to put on the Armor of God, protecting ourselves with our faith, truth, righteousness, and the gift of our salvation. Paul reminds us to never retreat, for any reason, because our coat of armor does not cover our backs when we run from the devil. We are encouraged to be steadfast when facing the devil and to vigorously put up a defense against his attacks.

As was previously mentioned, it is believed that Paul wrote the Epistle to Ephesus around the same time he wrote his letters to the Colossians and Philemon. It was clear that Paul intended for these letters to be disseminated so that His messages could spread to a larger audience. For that reason, the letters are written in a general, non-specific way so that they might be as inclusive as possible for broader audiences.

The letters to both Ephesus and Colossae were delivered by Tychicus. Biblical scholars believe that Tychicus served the apostle Paul as a personal attendant for the better part of ten years and became one of Paul's most trusted confidantes. Because he was a native of the Asia Minor province, and most likely from Ephesus, it was believed that Tychicus would also take the letters and deliver them to churches throughout the province. Paul's intention in sending Tychicus to Ephesus was so that he could relieve Timothy of his pastoral duties there, allowing Timothy to travel back to Rome to visit Paul. Tychicus was a gifted pastor, known for his ability to offer encouragement to the congregations of recent converts.

THE LETTER TO THE EPHESIANS

The Letter to the Ephesians
New International Version (NIV)
(Used by permission of Biblica, Inc.)

CHAPTER 1

Paul, an apostle of Christ Jesus by the will of God,
To God's holy people in Ephesus, the faithful in Christ Jesus:
2 Grace and peace to you from God our Father and the Lord
Jesus Christ.

PRAISE FOR SPIRITUAL BLESSINGS IN CHRIST

3 Praise be to the God and Father of our Lord Jesus Christ,
who has blessed us in the heavenly realms with every spiritual
blessing in Christ. 4 For he chose us in him before the creation
of the world to be holy and blameless in his sight. In love 5 he
predestined us for adoption to sonship through Jesus Christ,
in accordance with his pleasure and will— 6 to the praise of
his glorious grace, which he has freely given us in the One he
loves. 7 In him we have redemption through his blood, the
forgiveness of sins, in accordance with the riches of God's grace
8 that he lavished on us. With all wisdom and understanding,
9 he made known to us the mystery of his will according to his

good pleasure, which he purposed in Christ, 10 to be put into
effect when the times reach their fulfillment—to bring unity to all
things in heaven and on earth under Christ.

11 In him we were also chosen, having been predestined according
to the plan of him who works out everything in conformity with
the purpose of his will, 12 in order that we, who were the first to
put our hope in Christ, might be for the praise of his glory. 13 And
you also were included in Christ when you heard the message of
truth, the gospel of your salvation. When you believed, you were
marked in him with a seal, the promised Holy Spirit, 14 who is a
deposit guaranteeing our inheritance until the redemption of those
who are God's possession—to the praise of his glory.

THANKSGIVING AND PRAYER

15 For this reason, ever since I heard about your faith in the Lord
Jesus and your love for all God's people, 16 I have not stopped giving
thanks for you, remembering you in my prayers. 17 I keep asking
that the God of our Lord Jesus Christ, the glorious Father, may give
you the Spirit of wisdom and revelation, so that you may know
him better. 18 I pray that the eyes of your heart may be enlightened
in order that you may know the hope to which he has called you,
the riches of his glorious inheritance in his holy people, 19 and his
incomparably great power for us who believe. That power is the same
as the mighty strength 20 he exerted when he raised Christ from
the dead and seated him at his right hand in the heavenly realms,
21 far above all rule and authority, power and dominion, and every
name that is invoked, not only in the present age but also in the one
to come. 22 And God placed all things under his feet and appointed
him to be head over everything for the church, 23 which is his body,
the fullness of him who fills everything in every way.

CHAPTER 2

MADE ALIVE IN CHRIST

As for you, you were dead in your transgressions and sins, 2 in which you used to live when you followed the ways of this world and of the ruler of the kingdom of the air, the spirit who is now at work in those who are disobedient. 3 All of us also lived among them at one time, gratifying the cravings of our flesh and following its desires and thoughts. Like the rest, we were by nature deserving of wrath. 4 But because of his great love for us, God, who is rich in mercy, 5 made us alive with Christ even when we were dead in transgressions—it is by grace you have been saved. 6 And God raised us up with Christ and seated us with him in the heavenly realms in Christ Jesus, 7 in order that in the coming ages he might show the incomparable riches of his grace, expressed in his kindness to us in Christ Jesus. 8 For it is by grace you have been saved, through faith—and this is not from yourselves, it is the gift of God— 9 not by works, so that no one can boast. 10 For we are God's handiwork, created in Christ Jesus to do good works, which God prepared in advance for us to do.

JEW AND GENTILE RECONCILED THROUGH CHRIST

11 Therefore, remember that formerly you who are Gentiles by birth and called "uncircumcised" by those who call themselves "the circumcision" (which is done in the body by human hands)— 12 remember that at that time you were separate from Christ, excluded from citizenship in Israel and foreigners to the covenants of the promise, without hope and without God in the

world. 13 But now in Christ Jesus you who once were far away
have been brought near by the blood of Christ.

14 For he himself is our peace, who has made the two groups
one and has destroyed the barrier, the dividing wall of hostility,
15 by setting aside in his flesh the law with its commands and
regulations. His purpose was to create in himself one new
humanity out of the two, thus making peace, 16 and in one
body to reconcile both of them to God through the cross, by
which he put to death their hostility. 17 He came and preached
peace to you who were far away and peace to those who were
near. 18 For through him we both have access to the Father by
one Spirit.

19 Consequently, you are no longer foreigners and strangers,
but fellow citizens with God's people and also members of
his household, 20 built on the foundation of the apostles and
prophets, with Christ Jesus himself as the chief cornerstone.21 In
him the whole building is joined together and rises to become a
holy temple in the Lord. 22 And in him you too are being built
together to become a dwelling in which God lives by his Spirit.

CHAPTER 3

GOD'S MARVELOUS PLAN FOR THE GENTILES

For this reason, I, Paul, the prisoner of Christ Jesus for the sake of
you Gentiles—2 Surely you have heard about the administration
of God's grace that was given to me for you, 3 that is, the mystery
made known to me by revelation, as I have already written
briefly. 4 In reading this, then, you will be able to understand my
insight into the mystery of Christ, 5 which was not made known

to people in other generations as it has now been revealed by the Spirit to God's holy apostles and prophets. 6 This mystery is that through the gospel the Gentiles are heirs together with Israel, members together of one body, and sharers together in the promise in Christ Jesus. 7 I became a servant of this gospel by the gift of God's grace given me through the working of his power. 8 Although I am less than the least of all the Lord's people, this grace was given me: to preach to the Gentiles the boundless riches of Christ, 9 and to make plain to everyone the administration of this mystery, which for ages past was kept hidden in God, who created all things. 10 His intent was that now, through the church, the manifold wisdom of God should be made known to the rulers and authorities in the heavenly realms, 11 according to his eternal purpose that he accomplished in Christ Jesus our Lord. 12 In him and through faith in him we may approach God with freedom and confidence. 13 I ask you, therefore, not to be discouraged because of my sufferings for you, which are your glory.

A PRAYER FOR THE EPHESIANS

14 For this reason I kneel before the Father, 15 from whom every family in heaven and on earth derives its name. 16 I pray that out of his glorious riches he may strengthen you with power through his Spirit in your inner being, 17 so that Christ may dwell in your hearts through faith. And I pray that you, being rooted and established in love, 18 may have power, together with all the Lord's holy people, to grasp how wide and long and high and deep is the love of Christ, 19 and to know this love that surpasses knowledge—that you may be filled to the measure of all the fullness of God.

20 Now to him who is able to do immeasurably more than all we ask or imagine, according to his power that is at work within us, 21 to him be glory in the church and in Christ Jesus throughout all generations, for ever and ever! Amen.

CHAPTER 4

UNITY AND MATURITY IN THE BODY OF CHRIST

As a prisoner for the Lord, then, I urge you to live a life worthy of the calling you have received. 2 Be completely humble and gentle; be patient, bearing with one another in love. 3 Make every effort to keep the unity of the Spirit through the bond of peace. 4 There is one body and one Spirit, just as you were called to one hope when you were called; 5 one Lord, one faith, one baptism; 6 one God and Father of all, who is over all and through all and in all. 7 But to each one of us grace has been given as Christ apportioned it. 8 This is why it says:
"When he ascended on high,
    he took many captives
    and gave gifts to his people."
9 (What does "he ascended" mean except that he also descended to the lower, earthly regions? 10 He who descended is the very one who ascended higher than all the heavens, in order to fill the whole universe.) 11 So Christ himself gave the apostles, the prophets, the evangelists, the pastors and teachers, 12 to equip his people for works of service, so that the body of Christ may be built up 13 until we all reach unity in the faith and in the knowledge of the Son of God and become mature, attaining to the whole measure of the fullness of Christ.

14 Then we will no longer be infants, tossed back and forth by the waves, and blown here and there by every wind of teaching and by the cunning and craftiness of people in their deceitful scheming. 15 Instead, speaking the truth in love, we will grow to become in every respect the mature body of him who is the head, that is, Christ. 16 From him the whole body, joined and held together by every supporting ligament, grows and builds itself up in love, as each part does its work.

INSTRUCTIONS FOR CHRISTIAN LIVING

17 So I tell you this, and insist on it in the Lord, that you must no longer live as the Gentiles do, in the futility of their thinking. 18 They are darkened in their understanding and separated from the life of God because of the ignorance that is in them due to the hardening of their hearts. 19 Having lost all sensitivity, they have given themselves over to sensuality so as to indulge in every kind of impurity, and they are full of greed.

20 That, however, is not the way of life you learned 21 when you heard about Christ and were taught in him in accordance with the truth that is in Jesus. 22 You were taught, with regard to your former way of life, to put off your old self, which is being corrupted by its deceitful desires; 23 to be made new in the attitude of your minds; 24 and to put on the new self, created to be like God in true righteousness and holiness.

25 Therefore each of you must put off falsehood and speak truthfully to your neighbor, for we are all members of one body. 26 "In your anger do not sin": Do not let the sun go down while you are still angry, 27 and do not give the devil a foothold. 28 Anyone who has been stealing must steal no longer, but must work, doing something useful with their own hands, that they

may have something to share with those in need.

29 Do not let any unwholesome talk come out of your mouths, but only what is helpful for building others up according to their needs, that it may benefit those who listen. 30 And do not grieve the Holy Spirit of God, with whom you were sealed for the day of redemption. 31 Get rid of all bitterness, rage and anger, brawling and slander, along with every form of malice. 32 Be kind and compassionate to one another, forgiving each other, just as in Christ God forgave you.

CHAPTER 5

1 Follow God's example, therefore, as dearly loved children 2 and walk in the way of love, just as Christ loved us and gave himself up for us as a fragrant offering and sacrifice to God.

3 But among you there must not be even a hint of sexual immorality, or of any kind of impurity, or of greed, because these are improper for God's holy people. 4 Nor should there be obscenity, foolish talk or coarse joking, which are out of place, but rather thanksgiving. 5 For of this you can be sure: No immoral, impure or greedy person— such a person is an idolater—has any inheritance in the kingdom of Christ and of God. 6 Let no one deceive you with empty words, for because of such things God's wrath comes on those who are disobedient. 7 Therefore do not be partners with them.

8 For you were once darkness, but now you are light in the Lord. Live as children of light 9 (for the fruit of the light consists in all goodness, righteousness and truth)10 and find out what pleases the Lord. 11 Have nothing to do with the fruitless deeds of darkness, but rather expose them. 12 It is shameful even to

mention what the disobedient do in secret. 13 But everything
exposed by the light becomes visible—and everything that is
illuminated becomes a light. 14 This is why it is said:
"Wake up, sleeper,

   rise from the dead,

   and Christ will shine on you."

15 Be very careful, then, how you live—not as unwise but as wise,
16 making the most of every opportunity, because the days are evil.
17 Therefore do not be foolish, but understand what the Lord's
will is. 18 Do not get drunk on wine, which leads to debauchery.
Instead, be filled with the Spirit, 19 speaking to one another with
psalms, hymns, and songs from the Spirit. Sing and make music
from your heart to the Lord, 20 always giving thanks to God the
Father for everything, in the name of our Lord Jesus Christ.

INSTRUCTIONS FOR CHRISTIAN HOUSEHOLDS

21 Submit to one another out of reverence for Christ.

22 Wives, submit yourselves to your own husbands as you do
to the Lord. 23 For the husband is the head of the wife as Christ
is the head of the church, his body, of which he is the Savior. 24
Now as the church submits to Christ, so also wives should submit
to their husbands in everything.

25 Husbands, love your wives, just as Christ loved the church
and gave himself up for her 26 to make her holy, cleansing her
by the washing with water through the word, 27 and to present
her to himself as a radiant church, without stain or wrinkle or
any other blemish, but holy and blameless. 28 In this same way,
husbands ought to love their wives as their own bodies. He who
loves his wife loves himself.29 After all, no one ever hated their
own body, but they feed and care for their body, just as Christ

does the church— 30 for we are members of his body. 31 "For this reason a man will leave his father and mother and be united to his wife, and the two will become one flesh." 32 This is a profound mystery—but I am talking about Christ and the church. 33 However, each one of you also must love his wife as he loves himself, and the wife must respect her husband.

CHAPTER 6

Children, obey your parents in the Lord, for this is right. 2 "Honor your father and mother"—which is the first commandment with a promise— 3 "so that it may go well with you and that you may enjoy long life on the earth."
4 Fathers, do not exasperate your children; instead, bring them up in the training and instruction of the Lord.
5 Slaves, obey your earthly masters with respect and fear, and with sincerity of heart, just as you would obey Christ. 6 Obey them not only to win their favor when their eye is on you, but as slaves of Christ, doing the will of God from your heart. 7 Serve wholeheartedly, as if you were serving the Lord, not people, 8 because you know that the Lord will reward each one for whatever good they do, whether they are slave or free.
9 And masters, treat your slaves in the same way. Do not threaten them, since you know that he who is both their Master and yours is in heaven, and there is no favoritism with him.

THE ARMOR OF GOD
10 Finally, be strong in the Lord and in his mighty power. 11 Put on the full armor of God, so that you can take your stand against

the devil's schemes. 12 For our struggle is not against flesh and blood, but against the rulers, against the authorities, against the powers of this dark world and against the spiritual forces of evil in the heavenly realms. 13 Therefore put on the full armor of God, so that when the day of evil comes, you may be able to stand your ground, and after you have done everything, to stand. 14 Stand firm then, with the belt of truth buckled around your waist, with the breastplate of righteousness in place, 15 and with your feet fitted with the readiness that comes from the gospel of peace. 16 In addition to all this, take up the shield of faith, with which you can extinguish all the flaming arrows of the evil one. 17 Take the helmet of salvation and the sword of the Spirit, which is the word of God. 18 And pray in the Spirit on all occasions with all kinds of prayers and requests. With this in mind, be alert and always keep on praying for all the Lord's people.19 Pray also for me, that whenever I speak, words may be given me so that I will fearlessly make known the mystery of the gospel, 20 for which I am an ambassador in chains. Pray that I may declare it fearlessly, as I should.

FINAL GREETINGS
21 Tychicus, the dear brother and faithful servant in the Lord, will tell you everything, so that you may also know how I am and what I am doing. 22 I am sending him to you for this very purpose, that you may know how we are, and that he may encourage you.
23 Peace to the brothers and sisters, and love with faith from God the Father and the Lord Jesus Christ. 24 Grace to all who love our Lord Jesus Christ with an undying love.

"Praise be to the God and Father of our Lord Jesus Christ!
In his great mercy he has given us new birth into a living hope
through the resurrection of Jesus Christ from the dead, and
into an inheritance that can never perish, spoil or fade.
This inheritance is kept in heaven for you, who through faith
are shielded by God's power until the coming of the salvation
that is ready to be revealed in the last time."

(1 Peter 1:3-5)

WEEK 1

THE CHOSEN FEW

Praise be to the God and Father of our Lord Jesus Christ. In Christ, God has given us every spiritual blessing in heaven. In Christ, he chose us before the world was made. He chose us in love to be his holy people— people who could stand before him without any fault. And before the world was made, God decided to make us his own children through Jesus Christ. This was what God wanted, and it pleased him to do it. (Ephesians 1:3-5)

'm always a little intrigued when I hear someone ask other people if they've invited Christ into their life. Given the fact that God specifically chose each and every one of us to be his children, I often wonder why the question of accepting Jesus is considered anything more than just a rhetorical question where the logical answer should always be a resounding, "YES!" Paul is telling us that the most significant reality is not whether or not we've accepted Jesus but that God, in Christ, has accepted us and that acceptance came long before we ever existed. The path to eternal life with God begins with a conscious decision to follow Him; however, the fact that you are a Christian is because God chose you to be one.

Our unique standing with God is an act of God's sovereign grace which means it comes from God alone according to His divine purpose. He has given us His grace and He will call us up when He returns. He will bring us through the toils, snares, and hard times in our lives, no matter how tough things get. Knowing and believing all of this should give us the confidence to be "all in" with God.

Are you living a life that honors God? There's no need to make an excuse for our lack of spiritual growth because of our struggle with sin, we've already been forgiven. Our ransom has been paid. Knowing that we were chosen before the world was made should empower us to be bold in our faith and to become champions of God's word. It is our responsibility in response to what He has done. Even though our salvation is a gift we don't deserve, we should, nonetheless, praise God for making it so. It is a privilege to be chosen as His holy children.

MY PRAYER

God, give me the wisdom to understand the enormity of what it means to be chosen by You. Empower me to live a life that honors You for the greatness of Your grace and one that inspires others to live by grace as well. Amen.

READ: JOHN 15:1-17

QUESTION #1: Do you believe that you've been personally selected by God to be among His children? If so, how does this change your perspective on the way you should live your life as a Christian?

QUESTION #2: What does it mean to be "all in" with God? What changes do you need to make in your life to reflect this?

CONTEMPLATE

Write about the changes you could make today that would allow you to live a life that more consistently honors God.

GOD'S FORGIVENESS

In him we have redemption through his blood, the forgiveness of sins, in accordance with the riches of God's grace that he lavished on us. With all wisdom and understanding, he made known to us the mystery of his will according to his good pleasure, which he purposed in Christ. (Ephesians 1:7-9 NIV)

One of the most difficult challenges I faced as a new Christian was coming to an understanding of the forgiveness that had been extended to me by God. When I recounted the long list of sins I had committed over the course of my life, I couldn't begin to fathom the notion that God was willing to give me a clean slate on the day that I sought His forgiveness and invited Him into my life. No matter how bad I felt about myself or my sinful past, God assured me of His unconditional love and invited me to become part of His family, not just temporarily, but for eternity.

In Romans 5:8, we learn that our salvation is not based on our good works, actions or even our attempts to live a life that is free from sin. Our salvation is based entirely on what Christ did. When He died on the cross, He washed away our sins and made it possible for us to have eternal life. Of course, Christ's sacrifice won't prevent us from sinning again; however, we should strive to lead lives free of the sin that creates a fellowship barrier between us and God. God hates sin, but our invitation to be part of His family is not conditional on our good behavior, nor will it be revoked.

As men, we must find ways to set aside our pride and independence so that we can accept God's incredible gifts of grace and mercy. Once we accept, we need to do everything in our power to become a good witness to Christ by living lives that are noticeably different from our sinful pasts. When we sin, as we will be inclined to do, we must be steadfast in confessing our sins and then asking the Holy Spirit to help us lead better lives. God will continue to demonstrate his intense love for us through His forgiveness of our sins.

MY PRAYER

God, thank You for Your amazing gifts of mercy and grace. Help me to make myself worthy of Your forgiveness and Your gift of salvation. Let me lean into the Holy Spirit as I strive to live a life that is pleasing to You and worth of Your unconditional love. Amen.

READ: ROMANS 5:6-11

QUESTION #1: What can you do today to extend the gift of God's mercy and grace?

QUESTION #2: Knowing that your salvation is based entirely on the sacrifice Christ made, what type of priority will you now place on doing good works?

CONTEMPLATE

What does it mean to you to be accepted into God's family?

PROMISE OF THE HOLY SPIRIT

And you also were included in Christ when you heard the message of truth, the gospel of your salvation. When you believed, you were marked in him with a seal, the promised Holy Spirit, who is a deposit guaranteeing our inheritance until the redemption of those who are God's possession—to the praise of his glory. (Ephesians 1:13-14)

A t some point in our lives, each of us has likely received a dose of unfair criticism from a loved one or a complete stranger. That's just part of life. Unfortunately, there are times when a critical word can leave a scar and plant a seed of doubt that sticks with us for the rest of our lives. Usually, the words that cause the most damage will come from someone whom we hold in high esteem like a parent, teacher, or coach. Even though those words were intended to simply get our attention, it's often impossible to shake them loose or the damage they inadvertently do.

Fortunately, we have an eternal father who has demonstrated an unconditional love for us; a father who will never criticize or condemn us. We are blessed that He has already made us part of His family. When we come into God's family, we get an unimaginable inheritance. Because He's chosen us to join Him in heaven, we get access to Him any time we want through the power of the Holy Spirit. We are also given his protection and the provisions we need because of His love for us. But most importantly, we get God's presence in our lives in the form of the Holy Spirit. God will never leave us nor forsake us. He is capable of meeting our every need. He is by our side every second of the day and night.

Another bonus of our inheritance is that God is NEVER angry with us. There is nothing we can do to separate ourselves from God and the promise he holds for us. We can take comfort in knowing God will help us make decisions, resist temptation, and give us direction and a sense of purpose. Knowing this, each one of us can proceed with confidence knowing that we are covered and protected by a loving and almighty God. Most importantly, He has given us the gift of salvation that will never be taken away because we are adopted into His family

MY PRAYER

God, thank You for including me in Your family. Give me the confidence to lead my life knowing that I have Your protection and that I have been given the spiritual gifts I need to love and serve others. Thank You for adopting me, O God, my strength and my redeemer. Amen.

READ: 1 PETER 1: 3-9

QUESTION #1: Can you recall a time when someone's words stuck with you for an extended period of time? How did that affect you?

QUESTION #2: How does the unconditional love of God compare to that of your earthly father? How is their love similar or dissimilar?

CONTEMPLATE

How would your life be different today if your earthly father treated you in a manner similar to your heavenly father? How would you likely feel about yourself?

OUR INHERITANCE IN CHRIST

I pray that the eyes of your heart may be enlightened in order that you may know the hope to which he has called you, the riches of his glorious inheritance in his holy people. (Ephesians 1:18)

A recent study on the Baby Boomer generation shows that these adults, born between 1946 and 1964, are set to inherit almost $23 billion from the estates of their parents. Unlike the Boomers themselves, their parents lived through the Great Depression, which motivated them to scrimp and save in fear that hard times might one day return. As Christians, we are blessed with an even more generous type of inheritance. Those who have chosen to follow Christ can expect to receive a blessing that far exceeds the value of all the wealth on this earth. Our nest egg is an eternal life with God in heaven.

Unlike earthly riches, our inheritance in Christ will never fade or be taken away from us. The value of eternity won't change with the ups and downs of financial markets nor can it be taxed by a government. Our heavenly inheritance is guarded by the almighty Father, himself. Our loving God has made sure it has been set aside and protected exclusively for us.

As God's adopted children, we have been given hope and assurance that good things are waiting for us once our days on this earth are complete. Knowing this, we can more heartily endure the trials we face. From 2 Corinthians 4:18, we are told to fix our eyes on what is unseen versus focusing on what is seen. The promise of what God has in store for us makes the waiting more worthwhile and meaningful. Those who have shared in God's suffering will also share in His glory. It all seems worthwhile when we keep our hearts focused on the ultimate prize of eternal life in the presence of God.

MY PRAYER

God, grant me the gift of discernment so that I might understand the inheritance You have planned for me. Let me fix my eyes on the heavenly reward of salvation You have set aside for all of Your adopted children. Amen.

READ: ROMANS 6:19-23

QUESTION #1: How does adopting an eternal perspective affect the way you view your worldly challenges?

QUESTION #2: What does it mean to focus on the "unseen" versus focusing on the things we can see?

CONTEMPLATE

How does your understanding of God's promised inheritance affect your view toward accumulating wealth and being financially secure?

BORN AGAIN

...made us alive with Christ even when we were dead in transgressions—it is by grace you have been saved. And God raised us up with Christ and seated us with him in the heavenly realms in Christ Jesus, in order that in the coming ages he might show the incomparable riches of his grace, expressed in his kindness to us in Christ Jesus. (Ephesians 2:5-7)

B ecause of the disobedience of Adam and Eve, we were all born into a sinful existence. This was done not by our own choice, but by a death sentence that dates back to the original fall of man. On the day that we were born, we were spiritually detached from God. We didn't have to work for it or earn it, and it was pre-arranged so that, in our fallen state, we would have no relationship with God. Our only hope for escaping this death sentence is to come to Jesus through our faith and seek the opportunity to be born again in Christ.

In our original birth, we were drawn to pursue passions of the flesh and all forms of immorality, impurity, anger, dissension, and envy. Our second birth, however, is accomplished only through the Holy Spirit. The regeneration of our spirit allows us to have eternal life with God. Through this rebirth, we are able to actively pursue God.

Thankfully, this process is not as complicated as it may seem. In the Gospel of John, we learn that anyone who hears the words of Christ and chooses to believe in Him will escape judgment and receive the gift of eternal life. It's just that simple. Through this gift, we can experience the kindness and generosity of our loving God. Through His grace, we are given a new life, one that is eternal and one where we are invited to live eternally as part of God's family in His glorious heaven. We have been called to pursue this new life with all of our hearts while leading others to know this same truth.

MY PRAYER

God, we come to You in thanksgiving for the incredible gift that is given to us through our regeneration from a life of death to a life filled with hope and promise. Let us seek Your grace and help others to do the same so that they, too, can enjoy the gift of eternal life with You. Amen.

READ: JOHN 1:9-13

QUESTION #1: What are the things that might cause you to be "spiritually detached" from God?

QUESTION #2: What are the barriers that might keep you from discussing with others a "second birth" in Christ?

CONTEMPLATE

Knowing that the promise in John 1 is true, how does this affect your willingness to disciple other men?

"This is how God showed his love among us: He sent his one and only Son into the world that we might live through him. This is love: not that we loved God, but that he loved us and sent his Son as an atoning sacrifice for our sins. Dear friends, since God so loved us, we also ought to love one another."

(1 John 4:9-11, NIV)

WEEK 2

BY GRACE ALONE

For it is by grace you have been saved, through faith—and this is not from yourselves, it is the gift of God— not by works, so that no one can boast. (Ephesians 2:8-9 NIV)

Have you ever received a gift from someone that was completely unexpected? How did you react? If you're like me, you immediately began thinking of ways that you could reciprocate or "earn" this act of generosity. Instead of simply saying, "thank you" and celebrating the joy of the moment, I tend to feel guilty, ashamed, and unworthy. In many ways, that's the same way that we have responded to God's gift of salvation. Instead of accepting the fact that God has wholeheartedly taken us into his family, we seem to fixate on finding ways to make ourselves worthy of His grace.

While our gift of salvation is indeed unearned, there is absolutely nothing that any of us can do to earn additional favor in God's eyes. God is hopeful that we will take His gift and find ways to serve others and build up His church. Paul stresses that our good deeds didn't earn us our salvation, but points out that our salvation allows us to perform good deeds. The fact that we are unable to earn God's grace further verifies that His love for us is truly unconditional. His love is steadfast, in spite of our sins and other unsavory behavior.

In Titus 3:4-8, we learn that God saved us, not for the good that we've done, but so that we could enjoy a life with Him that never ends. Imagine what it might be like if we embraced the idea of paying that forward? Instead of living in transactional relationships where there are debits and credits for everything we do, we should instead focus on giving all that we have to offer, expecting nothing in return. Isn't that exactly what God has done for us?

MY PRAYER

God, free me from my instinct to earn the love you have given me. Instead, let me focus my energies on loving others in the way You have loved me. Let me learn to give while no one is looking and do so for the joy and satisfaction that comes from serving You. Amen.

READ: TITUS 2:11-14

QUESTION #1: What are some of the ways you've attempted to prove your worthiness for God's grace?

QUESTION #2: What would your life look like if you shifted your focus to giving all that you have to give while expecting nothing in return?

CONTEMPLATE

Write about the relationships in your life that seem transactional to you. How can you change those relationships?

A WORK IN PROGRESS

For we are God's handiwork, created in Christ Jesus to do good works, which God prepared in advance for us to do. (Ephesians 2:10 NIV)

One of the most frustrating aspects of my Christian journey has been that my transformation has been anything but instant. Early on, I thought that once I made the decision to follow Christ, I would instantly act as a Christian should. I thought my temptation for sin would dissipate. To my disappointment, I am still a sinner in the first degree, afflicted by lust, greed, and selfishness. Even when I was intentional in my efforts to lead a more Christ-centered life, for every two steps I took forward, I found myself slipping back a step or two or more.

We can all take comfort in knowing that in God's eyes, we will always be a work in progress. It's a good reminder that the best part of the victory is the struggle. We ultimately treasure most of the things for which we've worked the hardest. Our spiritual growth is no exception. In fact, the process of growing spiritually is one of the most essential elements of our walk with Christ. In John 15, Jesus reminds us that He is the vine and we are the branches. Like a vine, we will require constant nurturing and pruning so that we can one day bear fruit. Without Christ, we are simply a branch that withers away.

We are God's workmanship, a thing of beauty that is full of promise for this world and for our eternal life with Him. To continue to grow, we must spend time in God's word and then listen intently to see what He is calling us to do. Even though I may become frustrated by the slow pace of the process, I can find comfort in knowing that I am growing closer to God every single day. When we are called to heaven, the masterpiece will be complete and we will be rewarded as good and faithful servants.

MY PRAYER

God, bless me with the perseverance I need to continue to grow in a manner that is pleasing to You. Let me embrace both the nourishment and the pruning that allows me to grow so that I may eventually bear the fruit of Your vine. Help me to appreciate the struggle as much as I enjoy the reward that comes in serving You. Amen.

READ: ROMANS 8:18-25

QUESTION #1: In what ways have you struggled to become a better Christian? In what part of your life do you struggle most?

QUESTION #2: How are you growing closer to God? In what areas of your life do you recognize the greatest change?

CONTEMPLATE

How does knowing that you are the product of God's workmanship affect the way you think about yourself?

SEEKING PEACE

*For he himself is our peace, who has made the two groups one and has
destroyed the barrier, the dividing wall of hostility. (Ephesians 2:14 NIV)*

The divide that existed between the Jews and Gentiles in early times
is eerily similar to the division that has existed for more than two
centuries between whites and blacks in North America and South
Africa. The same type of tension exists in the Middle East between the
Israelis and Palestinians. In remote parts of the world, we still read of
racial genocide and irreconcilable differences between disparate groups of
people. Sociologists suggest that conflict is an inherent part of the human
condition. It is as if it is contrary to human nature for us to live in peace
with one another. As Christians, we must embrace peace and know it is
only possible through Christ and that it is the fruit of the Holy Spirit.

Sadly, our sinful nature has us at war with God from the moment we
are born. In Philippians 4:7, we learn of a peace that transcends and
surpasses all understanding. This peace was introduced to mankind
at the birth of Jesus Christ when a host of angels proclaimed, "peace
on earth and goodwill to all who find favor in God." From that point
forward, Christ became the peacemaker whose own sacrifice made it
possible for there to be peace once again between God and man and
between people. If we are seeking peace in our lives, we would be wise
to seek Christ first.

The separation between the Jews and Gentiles was mainly due to
cultural differences and the belief among Jews that Gentiles were an
unclean people. The Apostle Paul and early church leaders promoted

common ground between the two. This peace would not have been possible without Jesus nor would the growth of Christianity been possible without the Gentiles. While the circumstances may be minor in comparison, we all have barriers in our lives that need to be broken down so that peace can exist. Shouldn't that process start today? Barriers separate, but peace unites.

MY PRAYER

God, cure my innate tendency to stir up conflict and let me seek the peace that is only available through Christ. Where there are differences, let me seek common ground so that I can follow Christ's footsteps as a peacemaker. Amen.

READ: JOHN 13:34

QUESTION #1: Who are the people in your life with whom you need to seek reconciliation.

QUESTION #2: What are the barriers that keep you from being a peacemaker?

CONTEMPLATE

Write about the areas in your life where conflict may exist today. What steps can you take to break down the barriers so that peace may be possible?

THE DEPTH OF GOD'S LOVE

...so that Christ may dwell in your hearts through faith. And I pray that you, being rooted and established in love, may have power, together with all the Lord's holy people, to grasp how wide and long and high and deep is the love of Christ, and to know this love that surpasses knowledge—that you may be filled to the measure of all the fullness of God. (Ephesians 3:17-19)

It's nearly impossible to fully comprehend the depth of God's love for us. Our individual understanding of the meaning of love is, unfortunately, based on the love we have experienced only by earthly measures. While most of us feel like we can understand or relate to the unconditional love that a parent has for a child, we don't fully comprehend that this love pales in comparison to what God feels for us.

Loving others is perhaps among our most difficult challenges on this earth. Most of us live by the Old Testament philosophy of "an eye for an eye," meaning that if someone has wronged us in any way, we are entitled to get revenge. It is our depraved nature, as men, to keep score in nearly every aspect of our lives. It's also against our instinctual nature to walk away from a fight. Beyond simply turning the other cheek, we are called to extend the love and forgiveness to others that have been graciously extended to us in Christ. To fully experience the perfect love that God has for us, we must graciously receive His unconditional love and then extend that love to others unconditionally.

In 1 John 4, we learn more about God's deep love for us. The fact that God sent His only son to die on the cross so that our sins would be forgiven is the most vivid testament of His love. We are told that we can't possibly begin to love God as much as He loves us but we can show our love for God by loving one another. God's love is brought to perfection when we love others.

MY PRAYER
God, teach me the ways of your perfect love. Rid my heart of the hate, resentment, and prejudice that I feel towards others. Help me to recognize others as Your creation, worthy of love in every way. Amen.

READ: 1 JOHN 4:7-21

QUESTION #1: In what ways does your love for others fall short of what God expects?

QUESTION #2: What are the circumstances or relationships in your life in which you tend to keep score?

CONTEMPLATE

Write about the ways that you can demonstrate the love you have for God.

THE INCOMPARABLE POWER OF GOD

Now to him who is able to do immeasurably more than all we ask or imagine, according to his power that is at work within us, to him be glory in the church and in Christ Jesus throughout all generations, forever and ever! Amen. (Ephesians 3:20-21 NIV)

Throughout scripture, we read of many instances where the miraculous power of God was on display. From the creation of the universe to the parting of the Red Sea to the resurrection of Jesus after the crucifixion, we know that we serve an almighty God. It's easy to be overwhelmed by the miracles described in scripture that were performed more than 2,000 years ago. Imagine all the miracles that God has performed since the resurrection of Christ. In Matthew 19:36, we are reminded that all things are possible through God.

As Christians, our lives could be infinitely better if we would learn to rely on and trust in the power of God more consistently. God's power is beyond our earthly comprehension. Paul tells us that we can live with the assurance that God can do immeasurably more than anything we can imagine. Imagine if our minds were constantly fixed on the power of God's love to work within us? Rather than seeking God's wisdom only when we are troubled, what if we were to seek His guidance and direction through even the most mundane tasks of our lives?

Because of God's immense love for us, He is committed to accomplishing all that is good in our lives. In Romans 8:28 we learn that our loving God works for the good of those who believe in Him and those who are called to His purpose. And what is that purpose?

54

He wants us to become increasingly like His Son (Romans 8:29). Understanding and embracing the magnitude of the incomparable power of God gives us the confidence to follow the spiritual promptings that urge us to love and serve others. Our lives will be exponentially better once we come to terms with the idea that all things are truly possible through God.

MY PRAYER

God, help me to grasp Your incomparable power and Your desire to use that power for good in my life. Open my eyes so that I might understand Your love for me. Embolden me to share Your love with others so that all will come to see and experience the goodness that You long to share with your children. Amen.

READ: JOB 26:7-14

QUESTION #1: What are the "mundane" moments in your life when you could stop and pay attention to what God is speaking into your life?

QUESTION #2: What are the "spiritual promptings" you might have suppressed because of other distractions in your life?

CONTEMPLATE

In your own words, describe a situation where you have witnessed what must have been the power of God.

"The seed that fell among thorns stands for those who hear, but as they go on their way they are choked by life's worries, riches and pleasures, and they do not mature. But the seed on good soil stands for those with a noble and good heart, who hear the word, retain it, and by persevering produce a crop."

(Luke 8:14-15)

WEEK 3

PRACTICING TOLERANCE

Be completely humble and gentle; be patient, bearing with one another in love. (Ephesians 4:2)

The concept of tolerance, fully explored, can be a double-edged sword for many Christians. We now live in a society where popular culture encourages having an appreciation for all opinions and lifestyles. Secular schools teach our children to treat all behaviors as acceptable with no regard to the sinfulness of that particular behavior. Unfortunately, this worldly tolerance often conflicts with our Biblically-based principles. The best way to find a balance between these two worlds is to first treat other's preferences and opinions with gentleness and respect and then to decide whether or not to share God's truth as it relates to the situation.

Perhaps our best example of tolerance was modeled by Christ who exhibited deep compassion for those who were lost including prostitutes and tax collectors. While He did not excuse sin or condone ungodly behaviors, He always found a way to show love before gently delivering God's truth. Jesus may also have been our best example of demonstrating intolerance. When Jesus went into the temple and turned over the tables belonging to the money changers, he displayed a level of intolerance or, as some would say, righteous indignation. In Matthew 7:13-14, Jesus describes a broad gate on a road that led to destruction and a narrow gate on the road that led to eternal life. Jesus never sacrificed truth to extend love, nor did Jesus withhold love to communicate truth.

Too often, being tolerant means compromising our values and bending our core beliefs. In Matthew 6:24, Jesus makes it clear that we cannot serve two masters. We should not be tolerant of sinful behaviors. However, we can use compassion and gently instruct to help the lost overcome their sins. It all begins with love. Through humility, we know that but for the grace of God, we too might be afflicted with an indiscriminate appetite for sin. Through patience and understanding, we can help expand God's kingdom.

MY PRAYER

God, give me the humility and patience I need to discern when to be tolerant and when to take a stand on behalf of Your kingdom. Help me approach every situation with love and understanding. Inspire me to be more like Jesus when I encounter sinful behaviors, both mine and those of others. Amen.

READ: ROMANS 14:1-4

QUESTION #1: What are some of the ways you can show tolerance and love to someone who is living a sinful life?

QUESTION #2: Can you show love and acceptance to this person without compromising your own values? If so, how?

CONTEMPLATE

Describe a situation where you bent your core beliefs for the sake of being tolerant. Did you miss an opportunity to expand God's kingdom in this situation? Why or why not?

CALLED TOGETHER

There is one body and one Spirit, just as you were called to one hope when you were called; one Lord, one faith, one baptism; one God and Father of all, who is over all and through all and in all. (Ephesians 4:4-6 NIV)

I t should be no surprise to anyone that we are living in a divided society. From the national political climate to doctrinal beliefs to things as silly as sports rivalries, we often find ourselves taking polarizing positions on matters of little importance. On top of these differences, we men are afflicted by a primal desire to be competitive. Since the earliest days of our childhoods, we've been programmed to want to be the fastest and strongest, to own the most toys and to have the most beautiful woman hanging on our arm. For most of us, life has been all about winning.

Unfortunately, this quest to be superior has inadvertently affected our self-esteem and put a strain on our most intimate relationships. More importantly, it has also driven a wedge between us and God. We've turned our possessions and passions into modern-day idols. Instead of loving our neighbor, we've chosen to treat them as if they were our competitors. We still struggle to live in unity with one another.

In his letter to the Ephesians, Paul was deeply concerned about the divide between Jews and Gentiles. Because human nature is at play, the divide between classes and races has evolved little in the centuries that have passed. In divisive times, we need the occasional reminder that the importance of those things that unite us are far greater than the little things that divide us. We can accomplish many great things when we work together for a common good. Imagine how we might change the world if we could find a way to set aside our differences and focus our energies on serving God by serving others.

MY PRAYER

God, give me the courage to set aside my ambitions so that I can find common ground with those around me. Help me to love those with different beliefs and to find and embrace the unique qualities of other people. Let me shift my focus from the things that divide us to the things that unite us. Let me do so in Your name and honor. Amen.

READ: ROMANS 12:3-8

QUESTION #1: What are the issues that have driven a wedge between you and someone with whom you were once close?

QUESTION #2: What is an area of your life where you are inappropriately competitive? How can you change that behavior?

CONTEMPLATE

Write about a common goal you likely share with someone with whom you may be currently estranged. How can you leverage that common goal to build a new relationship with that person?

GROWING SPIRITUALLY

Then we will no longer be infants, tossed back and forth by the waves, and blown here and there by every wind of teaching and by the cunning and craftiness of people in their deceitful scheming. Instead, speaking the truth in love, we will grow to become in every respect the mature body of him who is the head, that is, Christ. (Ephesians 4: 14-15)

One of the first steps towards Christian maturity requires making certain our actions and deeds align with the core beliefs we profess to follow as Christians. We can actually do more harm than good in our efforts to bring others to Christ when our behavior is inconsistent with who and what we claim to be. Growing as a follower of Christ means embracing the truths of who I am in Christ and then I will become more sensitive to sin and those truths will shape my behavior. We know that we are maturing when our hearts begin to soften for others, when we resist temptation and when we step away from sin like greed, pride, lust, and envy.

It's common to question our own spiritual maturity. Our inability to understand scripture and the significance of Biblical history in its proper context feeds that insecurity. As a result, we let our self-doubt keep us from engaging others in meaningful dialogue. Our confidence in these areas would grow if we committed ourselves to spend time in God's word every day. God wants us to grow spiritually and set aside our sinful behavior.

In Colossians 1: 9-10, Paul tells us to be "filled with the knowledge of God's will in all spiritual wisdom and understanding, so as to walk in a manner worthy of the Lord, fully pleasing to him, bearing fruit in every good work and increasing in the knowledge of God." We have been called to set aside our childish ways and to grow in our love for God through prayer and good works. Growing spiritually in Christ is a process that takes time, discipline, and obedience. God will be pleased by our efforts to grow, no matter how slow the process.

MY PRAYER

God, instill in me an earnest desire to mature as a Christian. Give me the confidence to recognize my progress and the discernment to know when I am falling short of serving and loving You. Let me demonstrate my growth, not by mere words, but by my actions in all that I do. Amen.

READ: COLOSSIANS 1:9-14

QUESTION #1: What are some of the practices that you can incorporate into your daily routine that will help promote your spiritual growth?

QUESTION #2: What are some of your current behaviors that might be considered to be inconsistent with those of a mature Christian?

CONTEMPLATE

Write about a time when your actions did not match your faith. How did that experience shape your Christian walk? What do you regret most about that experience?

A TRANSFORMED LIFE

You were taught, with regard to your former way of life, to put off your old self, which is being corrupted by its deceitful desires; to be made new in the attitude of your minds; and to put on the new self, created to be like God in true righteousness and holiness. (Ephesians 4:22-24)

A t some point in our spiritual journeys, we make a conscious decision to walk away from our old life and commit ourselves to live a life that honors God. Often this transformation requires us to be intentional about every action we take and every thought we have. We have become so deeply rooted in our sinful ways that we've forgotten that our actions and thoughts do not honor or please God. Sooner or later, we realize that life, as we once knew it, no longer works and we are motivated to pursue God and live a Christ-centered life. Unfortunately, it's not as simple as flipping a switch or taking a pill.

Living a transformed life is hard work but the reward is great. In Romans 12:2, we are encouraged to be transformed by the renewing of our minds so that we can live out God's will in our lives. Our thinking needs to change, not just our behavior. We must be renewed in the attitude of our minds. This is such a remarkable promise to those who are willing to change their ways and stand up to the forces of evil. Going along with societal norms threatens our intimacy with God. God wants us to be unique and to avoid the ways of this world.

Our earthly desires and ambitions might seem normal when we compare ourselves to others but, unfortunately, we live in a world that is deeply rooted in sin. That's one of the reasons God wants us to "hate" this world and focus our energies on the rewards that come with eternal life. To honor this promise, God has set aside an inheritance for us that exceeds our wildest imaginations. The earthly comforts we so desperately pursue today will seem irrelevant in comparison to the wonders of God's kingdom.

MY PRAYER

God, let me focus my eyes and my heart on living a life that honors You. Give me the discipline to resist the distractions and snares that the Evil One uses to pull me away from You. Let me be transformed so that I can live a life that honors You. Amen.

READ: 2 CORINTHIANS 5:16-21

QUESTION #1: What has been the most challenging aspect in the transformation of your old life to a new, Christ-centered life?

QUESTION #2: What does Paul mean when he refers to the "renewing of your mind?" How might this change your life and affect your Christian journey?

CONTEMPLATE

Write about the habits or practices that were part of your old life. How difficult has it been to walk away from the things that once defined you? Under what circumstances have you been more successful than not?

THE VALUE OF INTEGRITY

Therefore each of you must put off falsehood and speak truthfully to your neighbor, for we are all members of one body. (Ephesians 4:25)

ave you ever been caught in a lie? Maybe it wasn't your intention to mislead or misrepresent the truth, but when all was said and done, you still told a lie. Unfortunately, the damage is done. Perhaps you've lost the trust of a friend or embarrassed yourself. In the end, you've caused someone to question your integrity. Worst of all, you've called into question the legitimacy of your Christian walk.

In Proverbs 20:7 we learn, "a righteous man who walks in his integrity; How blessed are his sons after him." It is true that a man's integrity may become his legacy. More than just providing an outstanding example for our children, society puts a high value on people who stand by their principles and for those who can be trusted. Once one's integrity is called into question, it's difficult to regain trust and confidence. We spend a lot of time talking about whether or not a certain politician or church leader can be trusted, but we too often fail to hold up that same standard for ourselves. Oddly enough, we seem to be strangely tolerant of exaggeration, white lies, and stretching the truth.

We're all imperfect humans and even disciplined Christians slip up and make mistakes. What's important is that we work to establish a pattern of integrity and begin to demonstrate the ways in which we should emulate Christ. In this world where moral values are constantly compromised, we have a unique opportunity to stand up and model what living a Christian life truly means.

MY PRAYER

God, help me to discern the difference between the fact and fiction that could come from my lips. Help me to be steadfast in choosing the path of truth and honesty when choosing my words. Let my words be as good as gold. Amen.

READ: TITUS 2:1-8

QUESTION #1: Have you ever been caught in a lie that may have only started as an exaggeration? What lesson did you learn from that experience?

QUESTION #2: Name the people in your life whose integrity could not be called into question. Who are the people in your community with that same attribute? What can you learn from them?

CONTEMPLATE

Write about a time when you felt your moral values were being compromised. How did you respond? What steps did you take to avoid being put in a similar situation?

"This is the message we have heard from him and declare to you: God is light; in him there is no darkness at all. If we claim to have fellowship with him and yet walk in the darkness, we lie and do not live out the truth. But if we walk in the light, as he is in the light, we have fellowship with one another, and the blood of Jesus, his Son, purifies us from all sin.

(1 John 1:5-7)

WEEK 4

ADDICTED TO ANGER

In your anger do not sin. Do not let the sun go down while you are still angry, and do not give the devil a foothold. (Ephesians 4:26-27 NIV)

Psychologists have been studying man's addiction to anger for generations and have come to the conclusion that our propensity to become angry is somehow tied to our feelings of inadequacy as protectors, providers, and lovers. Most of us who have any degree of self-awareness will admit that our anger is often triggered by those moments when we feel as if we're losing some sense of control over some aspect of our lives. Often, someone or something has threatened our sense of self-worth or has put one of our loved ones at risk. For far too many of us, our anger has become a permanent facet of our persona. Unfortunately, we've become addicted to the adrenaline rush that comes with being angry.

We also have a tendency to withhold love and affection from those who might need it most, our wives and children. We substitute love with our service as the "provider" or "fixer." Perhaps we withhold love because we feel no appreciation for our roles in bringing home the bacon or for being the one who always has to fix the toilet, television, or toaster. Deep down, we've somehow convinced ourselves that our love is insufficient or inadequate. It's easier to become angry than to work through the complexities of our unmet needs in our relationships.

Paul is not telling us that anger is sinful. Instead, he warns us to not let our anger lead to sinfulness. He encourages us to not act on our anger. Self-control is part of the fruit of the Spirit and an important deterrent to anger. However, it's not just about controlling our angry outbursts because it is also sinful to withhold love. Giving our loved ones the "silent treatment" is not self-control. We must look to God and what He says about us in His Word, and explore the root causes for our feelings of inadequacy. Are we living out our new identity in Christ? Once we fill that void, our need for anger will lose its power and we can once again reward our wives and children with the unconditional love they deserve.

MY PRAYER

God, help me to overcome my feelings of resentment, anger, and inadequacy so that I can give the unconditional love You have given to me. Give me the peace that comes from understanding that You have accepted me and that You only have good plans for me. Help me to more deeply love myself so that I may more deeply love others. Amen.

READ: 1 PETER 3:8-12

QUESTION #1: Recall a time when you were angry with someone close to you. How much did your feelings of insecurity or inadequacy cause to you feel that you needed to protect yourself?

QUESTION #2: Can you recall a time when you used words to criticize a loved one? When can you talk with this loved one to ask for his or her forgiveness?

CONTEMPLATE

Write about a time when you decided to withhold love from someone close to you. What was the end result? In what ways do you regret this decision?

THE POWER OF OUR WORDS

*Do not let any unwholesome talk come out of your mouths, but
only what is helpful for building others up according to their
needs, that it may benefit those who listen. (Ephesians 4:29)*

Words matter. Words can define us. Words can also destroy us. The power of words in our culture is astonishing. Our words can either be a blessing that builds another person up or they can be a destructive force that devastates a person, shattering their self-esteem and impacting how they will ultimately view themselves. God wants us to use our words to bestow blessings and give life. Unfortunately, our own insecurities can cause us to tear others down in our attempts to build ourselves up. Even though it may not be our intent, a careless comment can cause damage that could last for generations.

The biggest problem with our words of destruction is that we can rarely take them back. Once we've uttered a hateful thought, the damage is done. Despite our best efforts to reverse the damage, our victim intuitively believes that there was an element of truth in our utterance. In Psalms 19:14, David asks that his words find favor with God, "Let the words of my mouth and the meditation of my heart be acceptable in Your sight, O Lord, my rock and my redeemer."

A man's words too often reflect the content of his heart. We know from the teachings of Jesus, that the mouth speaks out of that which fills the heart. You've undoubtedly heard the old adage advising us to think before we speak. In Matthew 12:33-37, we learn that a good man brings out of his treasure what is good and the evil man brings out of his treasure what is evil. Do you want to be judged solely by your words alone? Knowing that God will justify us by our words should be all the motivation we need to use our words to build others up instead of tearing them down.

MY PRAYER

God, let my words be a true reflection of what's in my heart. God, cleanse my heart and make it pure, filled with love and a desire to bestow blessings on every person with whom I speak. Let my words be a light that inspires, encourages, and reflects my love for You. Amen.

READ: JAMES 3:3-12

QUESTION #1: Recall a moment from your childhood when a parent, teacher, or coach said something to you that has had a lasting impact. How did that one comment affect your confidence or world view?

QUESTION #2: Can you recall a time when you used words to criticize a loved one? When can you talk with this loved one to ask for their forgiveness?

CONTEMPLATE

Write about a time when someone's kind or encouraging words bolstered the way you perceived yourself. Recall the emotions you felt. How can you pay this forward?

SEEK RECONCILIATION

Be kind and compassionate to one another, forgiving each other, just as in Christ God forgave you. (Ephesians 4:32)

Most of us have long-standing conflicts that remain unresolved. Some of us have parted ways with old friends from high school or college while others have estranged relationships with siblings, parents, or other family members. True to human nature, many of us might have a tough time remembering the exact reason why we are estranged while others can remember the precise moment that trust was lost because a painful memory is seared deeply into our hearts and minds. We say we can forgive, but deep down inside we refuse to forget the transgression. We continue to carry a grudge with bitterness in our hearts.

In Matthew 18, we learn of the consequences for the unmerciful servant who refused to forgive a debt even though he was forgiven a far greater debt by his master. As Christians, we have been forgiven a lifetime of sins because Christ paid our ransom and made the ultimate sacrifice in dying on the cross. God is glorified when we pay it forward by forgiving those who have sinned against us. No matter how egregious the offense, we must find a way to dig deep and offer heartfelt forgiveness.

We can step away from the shame and guilt that holds us back by giving and seeking forgiveness. Once done, God is glorified when we take it a step further and seek reconciliation with those from whom we've been estranged. Our unresolved conflicts are keeping us from being free to love and serve those around us. Like chains around our ankles, our differences with others keep us from truly seeking God.

MY PRAYER

God, let me be inspired by the way You have offered forgiveness. Give me the humility I need to set aside my anger towards others so that I can show that I'm worthy of the grace I've been given through Your death and resurrection. Amen.

READ: COLOSSIANS 3:1-17

QUESTION #1: What are the estranged relationships in your life where forgiveness and reconciliation need to be extended?

QUESTION #2: What are the barriers keeping you from extending forgiveness in these relationships?

CONTEMPLATE

Write about a time when someone unexpectedly extended forgiveness to you. How did this act affect your relationship with that person?

OUT OF THE DARKNESS

In the past you were full of darkness, but now you are full of light in the Lord. So live like children who belong to the light. (Ephesians 5:8)

I n Paul's letter to the Ephesians, he reminds us of our lowly status before we were adopted into God's family. A life without Christ, from Paul's perspective, was like living in the darkness with each of us destined to fall victim to the powers of evil, with no hope for the promise that God offers. Before knowing Christ, we were destined to be pulled down by the sins of lust, sloth, and gluttony. Paul uses the analogy of light versus darkness, equating light to hope, encouraging new Christians to reflect the light of God in all that they do.

In the Sermon on the Mount in Matthew 5, Jesus teaches his followers to live in a way that they will become a light for the world to see, like a city built on a hill. We are to be a light for other people so that they, too, will see God's wonders and goodness. Wouldn't it be great if complete strangers knew we were followers of Christ simply by the way we treated others? We have been called to spread the Word of God and to live our lives in a manner that demonstrates we are deserving of the special relationship we have with Christ.

When we become Christians, we agree to submit to Christ and set aside the foolish ways that lead to sin. This transformation can be a struggle on many levels, but our diligence and perseverance serve as a powerful witness to others. Shining a light for others to find their way to Christ is the least we can offer our loving God. Our reward is the promise and satisfaction of eternal life with our Maker.

MY PRAYER

God, keep my eyes set on the prize of eternal life with you. Through my struggles and doubt, let me be that beacon of light for others to see. Let me lead and live my life by example so that others will follow me out of the darkness and into the light of Your Salvation. Amen.

READ: MATTHEW 5:14–16

QUESTION #1: In what ways could you reflect the light of God in your life?

QUESTION #2: In what ways could you demonstrate that you are a Christ-follower in such a way that people ask the reason for the hope that they see in you? (1 Peter 3:15)

CONTEMPLATE

Write about someone whom you believe is a shining light for others through their words, deeds, or actions. What is different about his or her life from yours? In what ways are you similar to that person?

A SPIRITUAL AWAKENING

This is why it is said: "Wake up, sleeper, rise from the dead, and Christ will shine on you." (Ephesians 5:14)

A t some point in our spiritual journeys, we will hopefully experience a moment where we suddenly recognize that our lives are better because we've surrendered control over to Jesus. Because we are born into sin, we walked toward destruction until the day God lifted us up and chose us to be His followers. The transformation that takes us from being lost in our sin to pursuing a life filled with hope is indeed a spiritual awakening. At that moment in time, we are born again into a new life.

The Apostle Paul experienced his own spiritual awakening while in the midst of his efforts to persecute Christ-followers. In Acts 9, we learn of the dramatic turn of events where Paul (then known as Saul) is traveling to Damascus and encounters the voice of Jesus in a bright light that temporarily blinds him. After three days Jesus sends a believer by the name of Ananias to Paul. Ananias lays his hands on Paul to restore his vision. From that point forward, Paul is transformed into a fervent believer who proclaims the fact that Jesus is the Messiah.

Our own spiritual awakening may not be as dramatic as Paul's, but we each have a standing invitation to rise from our spiritual death and become followers of Christ. Whether it's a personal tragedy or a joyous triumph that acts as the catalyst, the moment will be memorable. For others, the transformation may be a slow, intentional process encouraged by others guiding us to a new life. Whichever the case, it all begins when Jesus sheds His light upon us. Let us pray that God will use us to spread His word so that others can witness the light of Jesus.

MY PRAYER

God, let me be a catalyst of hope for those who are seeking you. Let the light that shines from me help others see You more clearly. Let my spiritual awakening be an invitation for all who seek You. Let my walk honor You in a way that inspires others to pursue You. Amen.

READ: ACTS 9:1–19

QUESTION #1: What was the sequence of events that led to your spiritual awakening?

QUESTION #2: How might you become a more intentional "catalyst" that helps others experience the benefits of following Christ?

CONTEMPLATE

Recall a time when you gained an awareness that following Christ made your life more complete. What triggered this awakening? Is this sensation sustainable? Why or why not?

"You are the salt of the earth. But if the salt loses its saltiness, how can it be made salty again? It is no longer good for anything, except to be thrown out and trampled underfoot. "You are the light of the world. A town built on a hill cannot be hidden. Neither do people light a lamp and put it under a bowl. Instead they put it on its stand, and it gives light to everyone in the house. In the same way, let your light shine before others, that they may see your good deeds and glorify your Father in heaven.

(Matthew 5:13-16)

WEEK 5

A LIFE-GIVING HUSBAND

Husbands, love your wives, just as Christ loved the church and gave himself up for her to make her holy, cleansing her by the washing with water through the word, and to present her to himself as a radiant church, without stain or wrinkle or any other blemish, but holy and blameless. (Ephesians 5:25-27)

In the early 1990s, a book called *Men Are From Mars, Women Are From Venus* was written to help men and women better understand the opposite sex. More than 50 million copies of the book were sold. The book was widely received because it shed light on key psychological issues that affect the interaction between men and women. Because of these differences, our marriages can, at times, be the most complicated part of our lives. Even though the roles of men and women in our society have evolved significantly in the last 30 years, there's still a great divide in how men and women communicate and react to situations.

Paul instructs us to love our wives in the manner in which Christ loved the church. Because Christ uses the church to help His followers walk with God, we can only assume that, as husbands, we also have an obligation to help our wives and families walk with God. Beyond simply being a provider, there's a more pressing need to lead our families and protect them from the evil in this world. Too often, our passivity prevents us from stepping up and protecting our loved ones from the decisions that ultimately hurt them. One only has to go back to the Garden of Eden to see how a man's passivity can affect a family tree for generations.

To have a happy marriage, we must embrace our differences and become intentional in how we serve and communicate with our wives. Our wives need to feel deeply loved and honored. Beyond just saying we love our wives, we must go further and demonstrate our love. A life-giving husband gives his wife reassurance, stability, and communicates with her in a manner that helps settle her fears and insecurities. Our wives should be able to derive comfort from us in much the same manner as we derive comfort from knowing Christ. A happy life begins with a happy wife.

MY PRAYER

God, let me love and serve my wife the way Christ loved and served His church. Encourage me to lead my family and to be assertive in protecting and caring for them. Help me to embrace our differences and focus on that which unites and strengthens my family. Amen.

READ: 1 CORINTHIANS 13:1-13

QUESTION #1: In what ways can you better demonstrate your love for your wife? How can you give her reassurance and comfort?

QUESTION #2: What lessons did you learn from observing your parents that might help you become a more loving and supportive husband?

CONTEMPLATE

Write about the blessings your wife brings to your marriage. Focus on the sacrifices she makes on behalf of you, your children, and your household. In what ways can you be more attentive to her needs and feelings?

HONORING OUR WIVES

In this same way, husbands ought to love their wives as their own bodies. He who loves his wife loves himself. After all, no one ever hated their own body, but they feed and care for their body, just as Christ does the church—(Ephesians 5:28-29)

I n his letter to Ephesus, Paul calls on men to love and treat their wives with compassion, mercy, and respect in a selfless manner. Though these words were written long ago, this advice transcends time even as the traditional husband/wife relationship has evolved with societal and cultural changes. Husbands are instructed to nurture their wives the way Christ loved and cared for His church. Paul emphatically stresses the importance of a healthy, loving relationship that should exist between men and their wives.

Some men, for example, dedicate a great deal of time to taking care of their bodies. While most men can't spend hours in the gym working out and sculpting their muscles, some simply have a strong commitment to paying attention to what they eat and watching how nutrition affects their bodies. For others, taking care of their bodies is an obsession. Regardless, God wants us to also pay careful attention to the well-being of our wives. He wants us to invest in our wives in the way we would invest in ourselves. Even if you're a couch potato or lead a sedentary lifestyle, the message is the same...love your wife more than you love yourself.

Christ's love for His church ultimately took him to the cross. Do you feel that same depth of love for your wife? Loving your wife should require some degree of sacrifice on your part. Through humility and respect, we are called to love our wives without reservation and without condition. Our heart's desire should be to make any sacrifice required so that our wives can become the women Christ desires her to be.

MY PRAYER

God, help me to become a better husband. Guide me to love my wife in the way you loved Your church. Prepare me to sacrifice whatever is necessary to protect and honor her. Amen.

READ: PHILIPPIANS 2:3-4

QUESTION #1: In what ways can you be more intentional in terms of loving your wife?

QUESTION #2: What sacrifice(s) are you willing to make to strengthen your relationship with your wife?

CONTEMPLATE

Write about the emotional needs of your wife. What are the things that make her feel valued in your marriage and in your household? What are the barriers that are keeping you from meeting that need?

A CALL TO OBEDIENCE

Children, obey your parents in the Lord, for this is right. "Honor your father and mother"—which is the first commandment with a promise— "so that it may go well with you and that you may enjoy long life on the earth" (Ephesians 6:1-3 NIV)

Since a very young age, most of us have been taught that obedience is important. As parents, we want our children to be obedient and follow rules because we want to protect them. God has the same goals for us. His desire to protect us from sin and our own foolishness is driven by his overwhelming love for us. Unfortunately, our pride leads us to believe that we can take care of ourselves and therefore we tend to push back when others try to influence our actions.

In John 14:15, Jesus tells us, "If you love me, you will obey what I command." From this, we should know that obedience is actually an act of love. More than submitting to the guidelines and rules of a higher authority, obedience is an act of worship, a demonstration of our faith. Obedience draws us closer to God. Paul calls us to submit to one another, regardless of our rank, social status or authority. This form of obedience shows respect and love where it might not normally exist.

In Ephesians 6:1-3, Paul is quoting from the Ten Commandments. God tells us in this commandment that the quality of our relationship with our parents affects our spiritual and emotional well being. It's a great conversation to have with a child or grandchildren to help them understand that God has placed you in their life to love them well. We must help them understand that sometimes loving them means keeping

86

them from doing something that we know will hurt or harm them, both now and in the future. This is why we ask them to obey. They can honor us by trusting that we have their best interests at heart. Likewise, we can honor our own parents by showing appreciation to them for loving us in the same way.

MY PRAYER

God, grant me the wisdom to be obedient in all that I do. Give me the clarity of mind to recognize the difference between Your will and my selfish desires. Let my obedience be an act of love that worships You and a heartfelt demonstration of my faith. Amen.

READ: ROMANS 6:15-18

QUESTION #1: What is the quality of your relationship with your children? What can you do to establish a more meaningful level of trust with them?

QUESTION #2: What is the quality of your relationship with your parents? What can you do to establish a more meaningful level of trust with them?

CONTEMPLATE

If obedience is an act of love or worship, how can you demonstrate obedience to your wife? What steps can you take to become more obedient to God?

PREPARING FOR BATTLE

For our struggle is not against flesh and blood, but against the rulers, against the authorities, against the powers of this dark world and against the spiritual forces of evil in the heavenly realms. (Ephesians 6:12)

I was skeptical when I first heard the term, "Spiritual Warfare." It was hard for me to believe that Satan had an army of demons working diligently to destroy Christ's church on this earth. The more I studied the topic, the more it sounded like a science fiction thriller. It wasn't until I had begun my walk with Christ in earnest, that I discovered the evil forces that were attempting to pull me back into my life of sin. The closer I got to God, the more intense the pull became. I began to witness, firsthand, a series of attempts to destroy my family, my business, and my life as I knew it.

At the precise moments in my life when my faith seemed to be at its strongest, a series of events would occur that would shake my faith. The devil's attacks were ruthless. My teenage son was in a horrific car accident. My wife was diagnosed with an aggressive form of cancer. My business suffered major setbacks. When I felt that I was at the end of my rope, a spiritual mentor directed me to Acts 18 where I read of Paul's struggles in Corinth. Paul, too, was under attack and in great danger for spreading God's word. In that dark hour, God encouraged Paul to be steadfast and to stand strong in the face of the enemy. I was inspired by Paul's steadfast behavior. I knew that I must also stand strong when under attack by the enemy.

I soon discovered that I had been uniquely equipped to stand firm in the face of evil. When I became resolute and focused on God, I miraculously gained power and strength over evil. I found immediate comfort in the Word of God and strength in His truth. When we put on the full armor of God, we can defeat evil with truth, righteousness, faith and the power of the Holy Spirit. In the end, our God endures, and we will all celebrate victory over Satan.

MY PRAYER

God, thank you for equipping me with the tools I need to defeat Satan and his attempts to destroy my relationship with You. Make me steadfast in this battle so that I might enjoy the promised rewards of Your kingdom. Amen.

READ: 1 PETER 5:8-10

QUESTION #1: Have there been points in your life where you have felt under attack by the Devil? If so, describe those experiences.

QUESTION #2: In what ways can you defend yourself from the attacks of the Evil One?

CONTEMPLATE

What does it mean to "stand strong in the face of the enemy?" What challenges would you expect to encounter? What are the things that would keep you from standing strong?

PROTECTED BY THE TRUTH

Stand firm then, with the belt of truth buckled around your waist, with the breastplate of righteousness in place. (Ephesians 6:14)

We live in a society where the definition of truth has become somewhat murky. We find ourselves questioning the integrity of news outlets, the validity of marketing claims, and whether or not we can still believe once "trusted" sources of information. In this era of social media, even the smallest kernels of truth are often exploited and distorted into a context that is no longer absolutely true. Unfortunately, most of us are either too busy or too distracted to research the veracity of a claim. As a result, we find ourselves living with a strong sense of uncertainty and doubt.

Paul tells us that the truth should always be the first line of defense. Without it, we are lost and susceptible to the schemes that could harm us. When we lack an understanding of God's truth, we become dangerously vulnerable. To defend ourselves, we must fortify ourselves with God's truth by spending more time in His Word. Once we are armed with the unquestionable truth, we can withstand any threat.

In John 14:6, Jesus tells us, "I am the way and the truth and the life. No one comes to the Father except through me." In these words, we learn that God, through Christ, is the personification and embodiment of truth. We know that absolute truth can only be found in God's Word. We can find comfort in knowing that all of life's answers are within easy reach. God's word is, after all, the very best place to find our peace, hope, encouragement, and now, the truth.

MY PRAYER

God, give me the discernment to know that the absolute truth can always be found in Your Word. Let me embrace Your truth and let it be my guiding force as I navigate life's greatest challenges. Let me, in turn, become an advocate for the truth so that all can find the peace that comes from Your word. Amen.

READ: PHILIPPIANS 4:8-9

QUESTION #1: Why do you suppose it has become so difficult to find truth in today's culture?

QUESTION #2: Is there one person in your life whom you can completely trust? How did this person gain your trust?

CONTEMPLATE

Write about a time in your life where you leaned into the absolute certainty of God's truth. Describe your confidence in knowing that the answers you were looking for were within easy reach. What was the outcome of this experience?

"Let your gentleness be evident to all. The Lord is near. Do not be anxious about anything, but in every situation, by prayer and petition, with thanksgiving, present your requests to God. And the peace of God, which transcends all understanding, will guard your hearts and your minds in Christ Jesus.

(Phillippians 4:5-7)

WEEK 6

PROTECTING THE HEART

Stand firm then, with the belt of truth buckled around your waist, with the breastplate of righteousness in place. (Ephesians 6:14)

When you picture what a Roman soldier must have looked like in his suit of armor preparing for battle, you begin to understand the strategic nature of the placement of each piece of armor. The breastplate was designed to protect vital organs, particularly the heart. You'll notice that Paul instructs us to put on the "breastplate of righteousness" so that we are prepared to do battle with the Evil One. As Christians, we are too often vulnerable because our hearts are not righteous and, as a result, we inadvertently let our guard down, allowing evil forces to strike where the most damage can be done.

We need to rely on the righteousness of Christ because ours alone is not strong enough to withstand the attacks of Satan. Once armed with this borrowed righteousness, we can begin to experience a transformation where we are empowered to live a more righteous life. When we stand in the truth of the gospel, our choices and decisions become more strategic and we become more battle-worthy to resist temptation and sin. When we seek refuge in Christ, we are using the gifts that God generously imparted to us when we became His children.

We must remain vigilant because the Devil is always searching for opportunities to prey upon our weaknesses. We are most vulnerable when we tolerate sin and rely on our own hollow sense of righteousness for protection. We can't accomplish anything without God. We must keep our hearts prepared and protected for battle. We are wise to be vigilant because Satan is relentless.

MY PRAYER

God, keep me ever mindful that my heart can only be made righteous through You. Let me absorb Your goodness every time I wear the breastplate of your righteousness so that my life will more closely resemble what You have planned for me. Amen.

READ: ROMANS 5:1–11

QUESTION #1: Why is it that our righteousness must be borrowed from God?

QUESTION #2: When do you feel most vulnerable to attack from evil forces?

CONTEMPLATE

Recall a time in your life when you felt completely heart-broken as the result of an event or situation. Describe the circumstances surrounding this event. What did you do to protect your heart from further attacks?

BE PREPARED

"and with your feet fitted with the readiness that comes from the gospel of peace." (Ephesians 6:15)

When I was a young boy, I joined the Boy Scouts of America. The motto for this organization, "Be Prepared," was drilled into our minds from my earliest days as a Tender Foot all the way through my final merit badge. On my way to becoming an Eagle Scout, I learned that the motto more broadly spoke to the importance of always being prepared in both mind and body for whatever life throws your way. We were encouraged to have the discipline, obedience and physical strength to properly contend with any unexpected circumstance or situation we might encounter.

In a like manner, Paul's letter to the Ephesians instructs his readers to have their feet fitted with the readiness that comes from the gospel of Peace. In other words, we must be prepared to lean into living out the message of the gospel in every area of our lives. Understanding God's truth equips us with the ability to know that we can stand firm knowing that His will and wisdom prevail in any battle. In addition to that, we will be protected by the truth that comes from being a child of God. The better we understand God's nature, the better prepared we are to do battle with those who want to pull us away from Christ.

Whether you're on the battlefield or ballfield, both a strong offense and a powerful defense wins the game. Using God's word to help others is an effective offensive strategy. When we actively speak of God's power and benevolence, we are gaining yardage into Satan's territory. Sharing the gospel message allows us to recruit more foot soldiers allowing us to gain traction in our efforts to make our way through life's most challenging battles. The gospel is our offense when we share it with others and our defense as we take our stand in the righteousness of Christ.

MY PRAYER

God, let me become a champion of Your word. Let me drink from Your cup of knowledge until I am adequately equipped to defend and grow Your kingdom. Let my days begin and end with a quest to better understand your ways and wisdom. Amen.

READ: 1 PETER 3:13-18

QUESTION #1: What steps can you take to become better equipped to stand in the power of the gospel?

QUESTION #2: What type of testimony can you share that speaks to God's power and benevolence?

CONTEMPLATE

Write about the opportunities you have had or will have to share the gospel with others. Do you feel adequately prepared to do so?

STANDING FIRM IN OUR FAITH

*In addition to all this, take up the shield of faith, with which you can
extinguish all the flaming arrows of the evil one. (Ephesians 6:16)*

Paul's analogy comparing a Roman soldier's shield to our faith
creates a powerful image. In Paul's time, a soldier's shield was the
approximate size of a door that could cover the soldier's entire
body. When a team of soldiers would advance towards the enemy in
unison with their shields placed together, they could literally form a
wall of protection. Paul's words are appropriately chosen when you
consider how powerful our faith can be when deterring the devil. When
we are fully committed to God's kingdom, we are much less vulnerable
to Satan's influence.

Simply believing in God is just one small part of what it means to have
faith. Scripture tells us that even the Devil believes in God. However,
this battle is about more than just believing in something, it's about
committing yourself. The right level of commitment requires putting
your faith in action so that others can see God's handiwork through
you. Our faith in God allows us to persevere through trials whether they
involve something as common as temptation or as difficult as suffering a
direct attack. Satan is powerless when our faith in God is strong and on
display for all to see. John tells us that "the one who is in you is greater
than the one who is in the world." (1 John 4:4)

As Christians, we are obligated to help others build a defense against
the Devil's work. It all begins with helping them understand God's truth
as it is found in His Word. We will be most effective when we walk side

by side with them as they explore, providing clarity and context where needed. The Devil is ruthless and persistent, always hoping to find us when our guard is down. Building a strong faith will help us protect ourselves and shielding others against his evil works.

MY PRAYER

God, help me to fortify my faith so that I can stand firm against evil. Let me help others protect themselves by sharing the wisdom found in Your Holy Word. Give me the strength to resist the Evil One with knowledge, strength, and perseverance. Amen.

READ: JAMES 1:12

QUESTION #1: Has there ever been a situation in your life where relying more deeply on your faith might have changed the outcome?

QUESTION #2: In what ways can you help others build a healthy defense against the work of Satan?

CONTEMPLATE

What do you foresee as the great challenges associated with protecting yourself and others from evil?

NOTHING TO LOSE

Take the helmet of salvation and the sword of the Spirit, which is the word of God. (Ephesians 6:17)

Have you ever been in a situation where it seems like you have absolutely nothing to lose? There are times when, in our minds, the consequences of winning or losing don't seem to be that far apart. If we succeed in our endeavors, that's great. If we aren't successful, the downside isn't really that awful. In Paul's worst-case scenario, he reminds us that we still have the gift of salvation. Paul's intent is not to cushion the blow, but to remind us that we can still move forward knowing God's plan has us covered for eternity.

Our salvation is the most generous and undeserved gift given to us by God. We have been pardoned from the consequences of our sin and still get to take a seat with God in heaven. No act of misfortune or evil can take away our salvation. Knowing this, we can take on evil forces knowing that we ultimately have nothing to lose. With confidence, we can be vigorous in our faith and bold in our actions. We can give a 150 percent effort, without fear.

We are called to be steadfast in our pursuit of God and to maintain an eternal perspective, even in the face of our most threatening challenges. Because our victory is won, we can overcome Satan's devious plan. Our helmet of salvation will help guard our minds against the threat of all our enemies. In the event our helmets fail, the other pieces of armor would become useless. The battle is first won in our minds. Once we have surrendered our mind to evil, the battle is all but lost. We must put on the full armor of God in the battleground of thinking to claim our victory in Christ.

MY PRAYER

God, keep my mind focused on the gift of salvation. Give me the eternal perspective I need to overcome the challenges presented by the Evil One. Keep me mindful of the truth that my battle has already been won. Amen.

READ: TITUS 3:3-8

QUESTION #1: How would having an eternal perspective affect the way you view the various challenges and obstacles in your life?

QUESTION #2: Has there been a time in your life where you lost sight of the victory you have already been promised? Describe the circumstances.

CONTEMPLATE

Write about the ways in which you can be more vigorous in your faith or bolder in your actions. Be specific.

PRAY ALWAYS

And pray in the Spirit on all occasions with all kinds of prayers and requests. With this in mind, be alert and always keep on praying for all the Lord's people. (Ephesians 6:18)

P rayer is an essential factor in winning spiritual battles. For that reason, prayer is not something that we do only as a daily ritual or when we're facing a desperate situation. In ideal circumstances, we should be in constant communion with God, praying without ceasing. The more we pray, the more our thoughts and actions can become aligned with God. The more we pray, the stronger our defense against evil forces. Not only is prayer an act of worship, but it's also an act of obedience. Submitting ourselves to God helps us to keep our lives in the proper perspective.

Praying also affords us the opportunity to share every aspect of our lives with God, asking for guidance and affirmation in the decisions we make every day. Prayer is the best way to express our gratitude to God for the many blessings we have in our lives, whether it's an answered prayer, a new day, a beautiful sunrise, or something as simple as a child's smile. Prayer is also our opportunity to regularly confess our sins and indiscretions, no matter how big or small. Seeking forgiveness keeps our mind focused on not repeating the sins we most often commit.

Prayer also allows us to prioritize our lives around God's desires. Consider praying when you are driving to work each morning. Pray when you are brushing your teeth, preparing a meal, or on your daily walk. As we grow in Christ, we will learn to pray as a habitual response to every situation we encounter, both good and difficult. Imagine the power that would come from turning to God along every step of our journey?

MY PRAYER

God, let this prayer and all my prayers be a reflection of the relationship I am building with You. Give me the inspiration and inclination to share my life through prayer while seeking Your guidance. Let me reap the harvest that comes from a powerful and meaningful prayer life. Amen.

READ: 1 THESSALONIANS 5:16-18

QUESTION #1: In what ways could you work prayer into your daily routines?

QUESTION #2: What are the barriers that prevent you from having a more consistent prayer life?

CONTEMPLATE

Prayer allows us to align our thoughts and actions with God. Write about the ways in which your life might change as a result of a more active prayer life.

15 RULES OF ENGAGEMENT FOR SMALL-GROUP STUDIES

1. Nothing said in the group gets discussed outside the group!
2. Be transparent. Be authentic. Be your true self.
3. Everyone needs to share, both as a speaker and a listener.
4. Encourage one another. Speak truth into each others' lives avoiding the temptation to "fix" each other.
5. Challenge each other. It's reasonable to disagree, but respect boundaries.
6. Give your darkest issues the light of day. It's incredibly liberating!
7. Be willing to be vulnerable. Take a chance and let your risk be rewarded.
8. We all have blind spots. Dare to explore what yours might be.
9. Absolutely NO gossip.
10. Embrace your mistakes. Take ownership of your weaknesses, knowing that we're all human.
11. Resist the urge to rescue others when they struggle to find the right words. Let people finish their thoughts.
12. Don't be afraid of silence. Pause and feel the weight of what has been shared.
13. Trust is our most important currency. Earn it and then be willing to extend trust to others.
14. Side conversations are not allowed; only one voice at a time.
15. When possible, find time to connect with each other outside the small group setting.

ADDITIONAL RESOURCES

FredParry.Life
Becoming The Man God Intended You To Be

Interested in using this book for a small group or Bible Study?
Visit our website for FREE study materials, discussion questions,
handouts, rules of engagement for small group participants, and
other teaching tools.

Want to offer feedback?

Write to Fred Parry, 711 West Broadway, Columbia, Missouri
65203 or email fparry61@gmail.com

www.FredParry.Life

CPSIA information can be obtained
at www.ICGtesting.com
Printed in the USA
LVHW100735061222
734654LV00011B/83